Date

Conditions

Weather

Terrain

Shelter

Shelter Constructed ☐

Type of Shelter

Clothing/Coverings ☐

Waterproof ☐

Animal proof ☐

Sunproof ☐

Fire Started ☐

Food Inventory

Rations ☐

Water ☐

Hunting ☐

Fishing ☐

Foraging ☐

Journey

Distance Covered

AF118647

Trail Markers Used

Landmarks Sighted

Animal Prints

Map Sketch

Lat. Long.

Party Member	Status	Injuries	Treatment

Date

Conditions

Weather

Terrain

Food Inventory

Rations ☐

Water ☐

Hunting ☐

Fishing ☐

Foraging ☐

Journey

Distance Covered

Trail Markers Used

Landmarks Sighted

Animal Prints

Shelter

Shelter Constructed ☐

Type of Shelter

Clothing/Coverings ☐

Waterproof ☐

Animal proof ☐

Sunproof ☐

Fire Started ☐

Map Sketch

Lat. Long.

Party Member	Status	Injuries	Treatment

Date

Conditions

Weather

Terrain

Food Inventory

Rations ☐

Water ☐

Hunting ☐

Fishing ☐

Foraging ☐

Journey

Distance Covered

Trail Markers Used

Landmarks Sighted

Animal Prints

Shelter

Shelter Constructed ☐

Type of Shelter

Clothing/Coverings ☐

Waterproof ☐

Animal proof ☐

Sunproof ☐

Fire Started ☐

Map Sketch

Lat. Long.

Party Member	Status	Injuries	Treatment

Date

Conditions

Weather

Terrain

Shelter

Shelter Constructed ☐

Type of Shelter

Clothing/Coverings ☐

Waterproof ☐

Animal proof ☐

Sunproof ☐

Fire Started ☐

Food Inventory

Rations ☐

Water ☐

Hunting ☐

Fishing ☐

Foraging ☐

Journey

Distance Covered

Trail Markers Used

Landmarks Sighted

Animal Prints

Map Sketch

Lat. Long.

Party Member	Status	Injuries	Treatment

Date

Conditions

Weather

Terrain

Shelter

Shelter Constructed ☐

Type of Shelter

Clothing/Coverings ☐

Waterproof ☐

Animal proof ☐

Sunproof ☐

Fire Started ☐

Food Inventory

Rations ☐

Water ☐

Hunting ☐

Fishing ☐

Foraging ☐

Journey

Distance Covered

Trail Markers Used

Landmarks Sighted

Animal Prints

Map Sketch

Lat. Long.

Party Member	Status	Injuries	Treatment

Date ____________

Conditions

Weather

Terrain

Food Inventory

Rations ☐

Water ☐

Hunting ☐

Fishing ☐

Foraging ☐

Journey

Distance Covered

Trail Markers Used

Landmarks Sighted

Animal Prints

Shelter

Shelter Constructed ☐

Type of Shelter

Clothing/Coverings ☐

Waterproof ☐

Animal proof ☐

Sunproof ☐

Fire Started ☐

Map Sketch

Lat. Long.

Party Member	Status	Injuries	Treatment

Date

Conditions

Weather

Terrain

Food Inventory

Rations ☐

Water ☐

Hunting ☐

Fishing ☐

Foraging ☐

Journey

Distance Covered

Trail Markers Used

Landmarks Sighted

Animal Prints

Shelter

Shelter Constructed ☐

Type of Shelter

Clothing/Coverings ☐

Waterproof ☐

Animal proof ☐

Sunproof ☐

Fire Started ☐

Map Sketch

Lat.

Long.

Party Member	Status	Injuries	Treatment

Date

Conditions

Weather

Terrain

Food Inventory

Rations ☐

Water ☐

Hunting ☐

Fishing ☐

Foraging ☐

Journey

Distance Covered

Trail Markers Used

Landmarks Sighted

Animal Prints

Shelter

Shelter Constructed ☐

Type of Shelter

Clothing/Coverings ☐

Waterproof ☐

Animal proof ☐

Sunproof ☐

Fire Started ☐

Map Sketch

Lat.

Long.

Party Member	Status	Injuries	Treatment

Date ____________

Conditions

Weather

Terrain

Shelter

Shelter Constructed ☐

Type of Shelter

Clothing/Coverings ☐

Waterproof ☐

Animal proof ☐

Sunproof ☐

Fire Started ☐

Food Inventory

Rations ☐

Water ☐

Hunting ☐

Fishing ☐

Foraging ☐

Journey

Distance Covered

Trail Markers Used

Landmarks Sighted

Animal Prints

Map Sketch

Lat. Long.

Party Member	Status	Injuries	Treatment

Date

Conditions

Weather

Terrain

Food Inventory

Rations ☐

Water ☐

Hunting ☐

Fishing ☐

Foraging ☐

Journey

Distance Covered

Trail Markers Used

Landmarks Sighted

Animal Prints

Shelter

Shelter Constructed ☐

Type of Shelter

Clothing/Coverings ☐

Waterproof ☐

Animal proof ☐

Sunproof ☐

Fire Started ☐

Map Sketch

Lat. Long.

Party Member	Status	Injuries	Treatment

Date

Conditions

Weather

Terrain

Shelter

Shelter Constructed ☐

Type of Shelter

Clothing/Coverings ☐

Waterproof ☐

Animal proof ☐

Sunproof ☐

Fire Started ☐

Food Inventory

Rations ☐

Water ☐

Hunting ☐

Fishing ☐

Foraging ☐

Journey

Distance Covered

Trail Markers Used

Landmarks Sighted

Animal Prints

Map Sketch

Lat. Long.

Party Member	Status	Injuries	Treatment

Date

Conditions

Weather

Terrain

Shelter

Shelter Constructed ☐

Type of Shelter

Clothing/Coverings ☐

Waterproof ☐

Animal proof ☐

Sunproof ☐

Fire Started ☐

Food Inventory

Rations ☐

Water ☐

Hunting ☐

Fishing ☐

Foraging ☐

Journey

Distance Covered

Trail Markers Used

Landmarks Sighted

Animal Prints

Map Sketch

Lat. Long.

Party Member	Status	Injuries	Treatment

Date

Conditions

Weather

Terrain

Shelter

Shelter Constructed ☐

Type of Shelter

Clothing/Coverings ☐

Waterproof ☐

Animal proof ☐

Sunproof ☐

Fire Started ☐

Food Inventory

Rations ☐

Water ☐

Hunting ☐

Fishing ☐

Foraging ☐

Journey

Distance Covered

Trail Markers Used

Landmarks Sighted

Animal Prints

Map Sketch

Lat.

Long.

Party Member	Status	Injuries	Treatment

Date

Conditions

Weather

Terrain

Shelter

Shelter Constructed ☐

Type of Shelter

Clothing/Coverings ☐

Waterproof ☐

Animal proof ☐

Sunproof ☐

Fire Started ☐

Food Inventory

Rations ☐

Water ☐

Hunting ☐

Fishing ☐

Foraging ☐

Journey

Distance Covered

Trail Markers Used

Landmarks Sighted

Animal Prints

Map Sketch

Lat. Long.

Party Member	Status	Injuries	Treatment

Date

Conditions

Weather

Terrain

Shelter

Shelter Constructed ☐

Type of Shelter

Clothing/Coverings ☐

Waterproof ☐

Animal proof ☐

Sunproof ☐

Fire Started ☐

Food Inventory

Rations ☐

Water ☐

Hunting ☐

Fishing ☐

Foraging ☐

Journey

Distance Covered

Trail Markers Used

Landmarks Sighted

Animal Prints

Map Sketch

Lat. Long.

Party Member	Status	Injuries	Treatment

Date

Conditions

Weather

Terrain

Shelter

Shelter Constructed ☐

Type of Shelter

Clothing/Coverings ☐

Waterproof ☐

Animal proof ☐

Sunproof ☐

Fire Started ☐

Food Inventory

Rations ☐

Water ☐

Hunting ☐

Fishing ☐

Foraging ☐

Journey

Distance Covered

Trail Markers Used

Landmarks Sighted

Animal Prints

Map Sketch

Lat. Long.

Party Member	Status	Injuries	Treatment

Date

Conditions

Weather

Terrain

Shelter

Shelter Constructed ☐

Type of Shelter

Clothing/Coverings ☐

Waterproof ☐

Animal proof ☐

Sunproof ☐

Fire Started ☐

Food Inventory

Rations ☐

Water ☐

Hunting ☐

Fishing ☐

Foraging ☐

Journey

Distance Covered

Trail Markers Used

Landmarks Sighted

Animal Prints

Map Sketch

Lat. Long.

Party Member	Status	Injuries	Treatment

Date

Conditions

Weather

Terrain

Shelter

Shelter Constructed ☐

Type of Shelter

Clothing/Coverings ☐

Waterproof ☐

Animal proof ☐

Sunproof ☐

Fire Started ☐

Food Inventory

Rations ☐

Water ☐

Hunting ☐

Fishing ☐

Foraging ☐

Journey

Distance Covered

Trail Markers Used

Landmarks Sighted

Animal Prints

Map Sketch

Lat. Long.

Party Member	Status	Injuries	Treatment

Date

Conditions

Weather

Terrain

Shelter

Shelter Constructed ☐

Type of Shelter

Clothing/Coverings ☐

Waterproof ☐

Animal proof ☐

Sunproof ☐

Fire Started ☐

Food Inventory

Rations ☐

Water ☐

Hunting ☐

Fishing ☐

Foraging ☐

Journey

Distance Covered

Trail Markers Used

Landmarks Sighted

Animal Prints

Map Sketch

Lat. Long.

Party Member	Status	Injuries	Treatment

Date

Conditions

Weather

Terrain

Shelter

Shelter Constructed ☐

Type of Shelter

Clothing/Coverings ☐

Waterproof ☐

Animal proof ☐

Sunproof ☐

Fire Started ☐

Food Inventory

Rations ☐

Water ☐

Hunting ☐

Fishing ☐

Foraging ☐

Journey

Distance Covered

Trail Markers Used

Landmarks Sighted

Animal Prints

Map Sketch

Lat.

Long.

Party Member	Status	Injuries	Treatment

Date ______

Conditions

Weather

Terrain

Food Inventory

Rations ☐

Water ☐

Hunting ☐

Fishing ☐

Foraging ☐

Journey

Distance Covered

Trail Markers Used

Landmarks Sighted

Animal Prints

Shelter

Shelter Constructed ☐

Type of Shelter

Clothing/Coverings ☐

Waterproof ☐

Animal proof ☐

Sunproof ☐

Fire Started ☐

Map Sketch

Lat. Long.

Party Member	Status	Injuries	Treatment

Date

Conditions

Weather

Terrain

Food Inventory

Rations ☐

Water ☐

Hunting ☐

Fishing ☐

Foraging ☐

Journey

Distance Covered

Trail Markers Used

Landmarks Sighted

Animal Prints

Shelter

Shelter Constructed ☐

Type of Shelter

Clothing/Coverings ☐

Waterproof ☐

Animal proof ☐

Sunproof ☐

Fire Started ☐

Map Sketch

Lat.

Long.

Party Member	Status	Injuries	Treatment

Date

Conditions

Weather

Terrain

Shelter

Shelter Constructed ☐

Type of Shelter

Clothing/Coverings ☐

Waterproof ☐

Animal proof ☐

Sunproof ☐

Fire Started ☐

Food Inventory

Rations ☐

Water ☐

Hunting ☐

Fishing ☐

Foraging ☐

Journey

Distance Covered

Trail Markers Used

Landmarks Sighted

Animal Prints

Map Sketch

Lat.

Long.

Party Member	Status	Injuries	Treatment

Date

Conditions

Weather

Terrain

Food Inventory

Rations ☐

Water ☐

Hunting ☐

Fishing ☐

Foraging ☐

Journey

Distance Covered

Trail Markers Used

Landmarks Sighted

Animal Prints

Shelter

Shelter Constructed ☐

Type of Shelter

Clothing/Coverings ☐

Waterproof ☐

Animal proof ☐

Sunproof ☐

Fire Started ☐

Map Sketch

Lat.

Long.

Party Member	Status	Injuries	Treatment

Date

Conditions

Weather

Terrain

Shelter

Shelter Constructed ☐

Type of Shelter

Clothing/Coverings ☐

Waterproof ☐

Animal proof ☐

Sunproof ☐

Fire Started ☐

Food Inventory

Rations ☐

Water ☐

Hunting ☐

Fishing ☐

Foraging ☐

Journey

Distance Covered

Trail Markers Used

Landmarks Sighted

Animal Prints

Map Sketch

Lat. Long.

Party Member	Status	Injuries	Treatment

Date

Conditions

Weather

Terrain

Shelter

Shelter Constructed ☐

Type of Shelter

Clothing/Coverings ☐

Waterproof ☐

Animal proof ☐

Sunproof ☐

Fire Started ☐

Food Inventory

Rations ☐

Water ☐

Hunting ☐

Fishing ☐

Foraging ☐

Journey

Distance Covered

Trail Markers Used

Landmarks Sighted

Animal Prints

Map Sketch

Lat. Long.

Party Member	Status	Injuries	Treatment

Date ____________

Conditions

Weather

Terrain

Shelter

Shelter Constructed ☐

Type of Shelter

Clothing/Coverings ☐

Waterproof ☐

Animal proof ☐

Sunproof ☐

Fire Started ☐

Food Inventory

Rations ☐

Water ☐

Hunting ☐

Fishing ☐

Foraging ☐

Journey

Distance Covered

Trail Markers Used

Landmarks Sighted

Animal Prints

Map Sketch

Lat. Long.

Party Member	Status	Injuries	Treatment

Date ____________

Conditions

Weather

Terrain

Shelter

Shelter Constructed ☐

Type of Shelter

Clothing/Coverings ☐

Waterproof ☐

Animal proof ☐

Sunproof ☐

Fire Started ☐

Food Inventory

Rations ☐

Water ☐

Hunting ☐

Fishing ☐

Foraging ☐

Journey

Distance Covered

Trail Markers Used

Landmarks Sighted

Animal Prints

Map Sketch

Lat.

Long.

Party Member	Status	Injuries	Treatment

Date

Conditions

Weather

Terrain

Shelter

Shelter Constructed ☐

Type of Shelter

Clothing/Coverings ☐

Waterproof ☐

Animal proof ☐

Sunproof ☐

Fire Started ☐

Food Inventory

Rations ☐

Water ☐

Hunting ☐

Fishing ☐

Foraging ☐

Journey

Distance Covered

Trail Markers Used

Landmarks Sighted

Animal Prints

Map Sketch

Lat.

Long.

Party Member	Status	Injuries	Treatment

Date

Conditions

Weather

Terrain

Food Inventory

Rations ☐

Water ☐

Hunting ☐

Fishing ☐

Foraging ☐

Journey

Distance Covered

Trail Markers Used

Landmarks Sighted

Animal Prints

Shelter

Shelter Constructed ☐

Type of Shelter

Clothing/Coverings ☐

Waterproof ☐

Animal proof ☐

Sunproof ☐

Fire Started ☐

Map Sketch

Lat. Long.

Party Member	Status	Injuries	Treatment

Date

Conditions

Weather

Terrain

Shelter

Shelter Constructed ☐

Type of Shelter

Clothing/Coverings ☐

Waterproof ☐

Animal proof ☐

Sunproof ☐

Fire Started ☐

Food Inventory

Rations ☐

Water ☐

Hunting ☐

Fishing ☐

Foraging ☐

Journey

Distance Covered

Trail Markers Used

Landmarks Sighted

Animal Prints

Map Sketch

Lat. Long.

Party Member	Status	Injuries	Treatment

Date

Conditions

Weather

Terrain

Shelter

Shelter Constructed ☐

Type of Shelter

Clothing/Coverings ☐

Waterproof ☐

Animal proof ☐

Sunproof ☐

Fire Started ☐

Food Inventory

Rations ☐

Water ☐

Hunting ☐

Fishing ☐

Foraging ☐

Journey

Distance Covered

Trail Markers Used

Landmarks Sighted

Animal Prints

Map Sketch

Lat.

Long.

Party Member	Status	Injuries	Treatment

Date ____________

Conditions

Weather

Terrain

Food Inventory

Rations ☐

Water ☐

Hunting ☐

Fishing ☐

Foraging ☐

Journey

Distance Covered

Trail Markers Used

Landmarks Sighted

Animal Prints

Shelter

Shelter Constructed ☐

Type of Shelter

Clothing/Coverings ☐

Waterproof ☐

Animal proof ☐

Sunproof ☐

Fire Started ☐

Map Sketch

Lat. Long.

Party Member	Status	Injuries	Treatment

Date ____________

Conditions

Weather

Terrain

Shelter

Shelter Constructed ☐

Type of Shelter

Clothing/Coverings ☐

Waterproof ☐

Animal proof ☐

Sunproof ☐

Fire Started ☐

Food Inventory

Rations ☐

Water ☐

Hunting ☐

Fishing ☐

Foraging ☐

Journey

Distance Covered

Trail Markers Used

Landmarks Sighted

Animal Prints

Map Sketch

Lat. Long.

Party Member	Status	Injuries	Treatment

Date

Conditions

Weather

Terrain

Shelter

Shelter Constructed ☐

Type of Shelter

Clothing/Coverings ☐

Waterproof ☐

Animal proof ☐

Sunproof ☐

Fire Started ☐

Food Inventory

Rations ☐

Water ☐

Hunting ☐

Fishing ☐

Foraging ☐

Journey

Distance Covered

Trail Markers Used

Landmarks Sighted

Animal Prints

Map Sketch

Lat. Long.

Party Member	Status	Injuries	Treatment

Date ____________

Conditions

Weather

Terrain

Food Inventory

Rations ☐

Water ☐

Hunting ☐

Fishing ☐

Foraging ☐

Journey

Distance Covered

Trail Markers Used

Landmarks Sighted

Animal Prints

Shelter

Shelter Constructed ☐

Type of Shelter

Clothing/Coverings ☐

Waterproof ☐

Animal proof ☐

Sunproof ☐

Fire Started ☐

Map Sketch

Lat. Long.

Party Member	Status	Injuries	Treatment

Date

Conditions

Weather

Terrain

Shelter

Shelter Constructed ☐

Type of Shelter

Clothing/Coverings ☐

Waterproof ☐

Animal proof ☐

Sunproof ☐

Fire Started ☐

Food Inventory

Rations ☐

Water ☐

Hunting ☐

Fishing ☐

Foraging ☐

Journey

Distance Covered

Trail Markers Used

Landmarks Sighted

Animal Prints

Map Sketch

Lat.

Long.

Party Member	Status	Injuries	Treatment

Date ______________

Conditions

Weather

Terrain

Shelter

Shelter Constructed ☐

Type of Shelter

Clothing/Coverings ☐

Waterproof ☐

Animal proof ☐

Sunproof ☐

Fire Started ☐

Food Inventory

Rations ☐

Water ☐

Hunting ☐

Fishing ☐

Foraging ☐

Journey

Distance Covered

Trail Markers Used

Landmarks Sighted

Animal Prints

Map Sketch

Lat. Long.

Party Member	Status	Injuries	Treatment

Date

Conditions

Weather

Terrain

Shelter

Shelter Constructed ☐

Type of Shelter

Clothing/Coverings ☐

Waterproof ☐

Animal proof ☐

Sunproof ☐

Fire Started ☐

Food Inventory

Rations ☐

Water ☐

Hunting ☐

Fishing ☐

Foraging ☐

Journey

Distance Covered

Trail Markers Used

Landmarks Sighted

Animal Prints

Map Sketch

Lat. Long.

Party Member	Status	Injuries	Treatment

Date

Conditions

Weather

Terrain

Food Inventory

Rations ☐

Water ☐

Hunting ☐

Fishing ☐

Foraging ☐

Journey

Distance Covered

Trail Markers Used

Landmarks Sighted

Animal Prints

Shelter

Shelter Constructed ☐

Type of Shelter

Clothing/Coverings ☐

Waterproof ☐

Animal proof ☐

Sunproof ☐

Fire Started ☐

Map Sketch

Lat. Long.

Party Member	Status	Injuries	Treatment

Date ____________

Conditions

Weather

Terrain

Food Inventory

Rations ☐

Water ☐

Hunting ☐

Fishing ☐

Foraging ☐

Journey

Distance Covered

Trail Markers Used

Landmarks Sighted

Animal Prints

Shelter

Shelter Constructed ☐

Type of Shelter

Clothing/Coverings ☐

Waterproof ☐

Animal proof ☐

Sunproof ☐

Fire Started ☐

Map Sketch

Lat. Long.

Party Member	Status	Injuries	Treatment

Date

Conditions

Weather

Terrain

Shelter

Shelter Constructed ☐

Type of Shelter

Clothing/Coverings ☐

Waterproof ☐

Animal proof ☐

Sunproof ☐

Fire Started ☐

Food Inventory

Rations ☐

Water ☐

Hunting ☐

Fishing ☐

Foraging ☐

Journey

Distance Covered

Trail Markers Used

Landmarks Sighted

Animal Prints

Map Sketch

Lat. Long.

Party Member	Status	Injuries	Treatment

Date

Conditions

Weather

Terrain

Shelter

Shelter Constructed ☐

Type of Shelter

Clothing/Coverings ☐

Waterproof ☐

Animal proof ☐

Sunproof ☐

Fire Started ☐

Food Inventory

Rations ☐

Water ☐

Hunting ☐

Fishing ☐

Foraging ☐

Journey

Distance Covered

Trail Markers Used

Landmarks Sighted

Animal Prints

Map Sketch

Lat. Long.

Party Member	Status	Injuries	Treatment

Date

Conditions

Weather

Terrain

Shelter

Shelter Constructed

Type of Shelter

Clothing/Coverings

Waterproof

Animal proof

Sunproof

Fire Started

Food Inventory

Rations

Water

Hunting

Fishing

Foraging

Journey

Distance Covered

Trail Markers Used

Landmarks Sighted

Animal Prints

Map Sketch

Lat.

Long.

Party Member	Status	Injuries	Treatment

Date

Conditions

Weather

Terrain

Shelter

Shelter Constructed ☐

Type of Shelter

Clothing/Coverings ☐

Waterproof ☐

Animal proof ☐

Sunproof ☐

Fire Started ☐

Food Inventory

Rations ☐

Water ☐

Hunting ☐

Fishing ☐

Foraging ☐

Journey

Distance Covered

Trail Markers Used

Landmarks Sighted

Animal Prints

Map Sketch

Lat. Long.

Party Member	Status	Injuries	Treatment

Date ______________

Conditions

Weather

Terrain

Food Inventory

Rations ☐

Water ☐

Hunting ☐

Fishing ☐

Foraging ☐

Journey

Distance Covered

Trail Markers Used

Landmarks Sighted

Animal Prints

Shelter

Shelter Constructed ☐

Type of Shelter

Clothing/Coverings ☐

Waterproof ☐

Animal proof ☐

Sunproof ☐

Fire Started ☐

Map Sketch

Lat. Long.

Party Member	Status	Injuries	Treatment

Date

Conditions

Weather

Terrain

Food Inventory

Rations ☐

Water ☐

Hunting ☐

Fishing ☐

Foraging ☐

Journey

Distance Covered

Trail Markers Used

Landmarks Sighted

Animal Prints

Shelter

Shelter Constructed ☐

Type of Shelter

Clothing/Coverings ☐

Waterproof ☐

Animal proof ☐

Sunproof ☐

Fire Started ☐

Map Sketch

Lat. Long.

Party Member	Status	Injuries	Treatment

Date

Conditions

Weather

Terrain

Shelter

Shelter Constructed ☐

Type of Shelter

Clothing/Coverings ☐

Waterproof ☐

Animal proof ☐

Sunproof ☐

Fire Started ☐

Food Inventory

Rations ☐

Water ☐

Hunting ☐

Fishing ☐

Foraging ☐

Journey

Distance Covered

Trail Markers Used

Landmarks Sighted

Animal Prints

Map Sketch

Lat. Long.

Party Member	Status	Injuries	Treatment

Date

Conditions

Weather

Terrain

Shelter

Shelter Constructed ☐

Type of Shelter

Clothing/Coverings ☐

Waterproof ☐

Animal proof ☐

Sunproof ☐

Fire Started ☐

Food Inventory

Rations ☐

Water ☐

Hunting ☐

Fishing ☐

Foraging ☐

Journey

Distance Covered

Trail Markers Used

Landmarks Sighted

Animal Prints

Map Sketch

Lat. Long.

Party Member	Status	Injuries	Treatment

Date ____________

Conditions

Weather

Terrain

Food Inventory

Rations ☐

Water ☐

Hunting ☐

Fishing ☐

Foraging ☐

Journey

Distance Covered

Trail Markers Used

Landmarks Sighted

Animal Prints

Shelter

Shelter Constructed ☐

Type of Shelter

Clothing/Coverings ☐

Waterproof ☐

Animal proof ☐

Sunproof ☐

Fire Started ☐

Map Sketch

Lat.

Long.

Party Member	Status	Injuries	Treatment

Date

Conditions

Weather

Terrain

Shelter

Shelter Constructed ☐

Type of Shelter

Clothing/Coverings ☐

Waterproof ☐

Animal proof ☐

Sunproof ☐

Fire Started ☐

Food Inventory

Rations ☐

Water ☐

Hunting ☐

Fishing ☐

Foraging ☐

Journey

Distance Covered

Trail Markers Used

Landmarks Sighted

Animal Prints

Map Sketch

Lat. Long.

Party Member	Status	Injuries	Treatment

Date ______________

Conditions

Weather

Terrain

Shelter

Shelter Constructed ☐

Type of Shelter

Clothing/Coverings ☐

Waterproof ☐

Animal proof ☐

Sunproof ☐

Fire Started ☐

Food Inventory

Rations ☐

Water ☐

Hunting ☐

Fishing ☐

Foraging ☐

Journey

Distance Covered

Trail Markers Used

Landmarks Sighted

Animal Prints

Map Sketch

Lat.

Long.

Party Member	Status	Injuries	Treatment

Date ______________

Conditions

Weather

Terrain

Shelter

Shelter Constructed ☐

Type of Shelter

Clothing/Coverings ☐

Waterproof ☐

Animal proof ☐

Sunproof ☐

Fire Started ☐

Food Inventory

Rations ☐

Water ☐

Hunting ☐

Fishing ☐

Foraging ☐

Journey

Distance Covered

Trail Markers Used

Landmarks Sighted

Animal Prints

Map Sketch

Lat. Long.

Party Member	Status	Injuries	Treatment

Date ____________

Conditions

Weather

Terrain

Food Inventory

Rations ☐

Water ☐

Hunting ☐

Fishing ☐

Foraging ☐

Journey

Distance Covered

Trail Markers Used

Landmarks Sighted

Animal Prints

Shelter

Shelter Constructed ☐

Type of Shelter

Clothing/Coverings ☐

Waterproof ☐

Animal proof ☐

Sunproof ☐

Fire Started ☐

Map Sketch

Lat. Long.

Party Member	Status	Injuries	Treatment

Date

Conditions

Weather

Terrain

Shelter

Shelter Constructed ☐

Type of Shelter

Clothing/Coverings ☐

Waterproof ☐

Animal proof ☐

Sunproof ☐

Fire Started ☐

Food Inventory

Rations ☐

Water ☐

Hunting ☐

Fishing ☐

Foraging ☐

Journey

Distance Covered

Trail Markers Used

Landmarks Sighted

Animal Prints

Map Sketch

Lat. Long.

Party Member	Status	Injuries	Treatment

Date ______________

Conditions

Weather

Terrain

Shelter

Shelter Constructed ☐

Type of Shelter

Clothing/Coverings ☐

Waterproof ☐

Animal proof ☐

Sunproof ☐

Fire Started ☐

Food Inventory

Rations ☐

Water ☐

Hunting ☐

Fishing ☐

Foraging ☐

Journey

Distance Covered

Trail Markers Used

Landmarks Sighted

Animal Prints

Map Sketch

Lat. Long.

Party Member	Status	Injuries	Treatment

Date ____________

Conditions

Weather

Terrain

Shelter

Shelter Constructed ☐

Type of Shelter

Clothing/Coverings ☐

Waterproof ☐

Animal proof ☐

Sunproof ☐

Fire Started ☐

Food Inventory

Rations ☐

Water ☐

Hunting ☐

Fishing ☐

Foraging ☐

Journey

Distance Covered

Trail Markers Used

Landmarks Sighted

Animal Prints

Map Sketch

Lat. Long.

Party Member	Status	Injuries	Treatment

Date ______

Conditions

Weather

Terrain

Shelter

Shelter Constructed ☐

Type of Shelter

Clothing/Coverings ☐

Waterproof ☐

Animal proof ☐

Sunproof ☐

Fire Started ☐

Food Inventory

Rations ☐

Water ☐

Hunting ☐

Fishing ☐

Foraging ☐

Journey

Distance Covered

Trail Markers Used

Landmarks Sighted

Animal Prints

Map Sketch

Lat. Long.

Party Member	Status	Injuries	Treatment

Date ____________

Conditions

Weather

Terrain

Food Inventory

Rations ☐

Water ☐

Hunting ☐

Fishing ☐

Foraging ☐

Journey

Distance Covered

Trail Markers Used

Landmarks Sighted

Animal Prints

Shelter

Shelter Constructed ☐

Type of Shelter

Clothing/Coverings ☐

Waterproof ☐

Animal proof ☐

Sunproof ☐

Fire Started ☐

Map Sketch

Lat. Long.

Party Member	Status	Injuries	Treatment

Date

Conditions

Weather

Terrain

Shelter

Shelter Constructed ☐

Type of Shelter

Clothing/Coverings ☐

Waterproof ☐

Animal proof ☐

Sunproof ☐

Fire Started ☐

Food Inventory

Rations ☐

Water ☐

Hunting ☐

Fishing ☐

Foraging ☐

Journey

Distance Covered

Trail Markers Used

Landmarks Sighted

Animal Prints

Map Sketch

Lat. Long.

Party Member	Status	Injuries	Treatment

Date

Conditions

Weather

Terrain

Shelter

Shelter Constructed ☐

Type of Shelter

Clothing/Coverings ☐

Waterproof ☐

Animal proof ☐

Sunproof ☐

Fire Started ☐

Food Inventory

Rations ☐

Water ☐

Hunting ☐

Fishing ☐

Foraging ☐

Journey

Distance Covered

Trail Markers Used

Landmarks Sighted

Animal Prints

Map Sketch

Lat. Long.

Party Member	Status	Injuries	Treatment

Date

Conditions

Weather

Terrain

Food Inventory

Rations ☐

Water ☐

Hunting ☐

Fishing ☐

Foraging ☐

Journey

Distance Covered

Trail Markers Used

Landmarks Sighted

Animal Prints

Shelter

Shelter Constructed ☐

Type of Shelter

Clothing/Coverings ☐

Waterproof ☐

Animal proof ☐

Sunproof ☐

Fire Started ☐

Map Sketch

Lat. Long.

Party Member	Status	Injuries	Treatment

Date

Conditions

Weather

Terrain

Shelter

Shelter Constructed ☐

Type of Shelter

Clothing/Coverings ☐

Waterproof ☐

Animal proof ☐

Sunproof ☐

Fire Started ☐

Food Inventory

Rations ☐

Water ☐

Hunting ☐

Fishing ☐

Foraging ☐

Journey

Distance Covered

Trail Markers Used

Landmarks Sighted

Animal Prints

Map Sketch

Lat. Long.

Party Member	Status	Injuries	Treatment

Date ______________

Conditions

Weather

Terrain

Shelter

Shelter Constructed ☐

Type of Shelter

Clothing/Coverings ☐

Waterproof ☐

Animal proof ☐

Sunproof ☐

Fire Started ☐

Food Inventory

Rations ☐

Water ☐

Hunting ☐

Fishing ☐

Foraging ☐

Journey

Distance Covered

Trail Markers Used

Landmarks Sighted

Animal Prints

Map Sketch

Lat. Long.

Party Member	Status	Injuries	Treatment

Date ______________

Conditions

Weather

Terrain

Food Inventory

Rations ☐

Water ☐

Hunting ☐

Fishing ☐

Foraging ☐

Journey

Distance Covered

Trail Markers Used

Landmarks Sighted

Animal Prints

Shelter

Shelter Constructed ☐

Type of Shelter

Clothing/Coverings ☐

Waterproof ☐

Animal proof ☐

Sunproof ☐

Fire Started ☐

Map Sketch

Lat. Long.

Party Member	Status	Injuries	Treatment

Date ____________

Conditions

Weather

Terrain

Food Inventory

Rations ☐

Water ☐

Hunting ☐

Fishing ☐

Foraging ☐

Journey

Distance Covered

Trail Markers Used

Landmarks Sighted

Animal Prints

Shelter

Shelter Constructed ☐

Type of Shelter

Clothing/Coverings ☐

Waterproof ☐

Animal proof ☐

Sunproof ☐

Fire Started ☐

Map Sketch

Lat. Long.

Party Member	Status	Injuries	Treatment

Date

Conditions

Weather

Terrain

Shelter

Shelter Constructed ☐

Type of Shelter

Clothing/Coverings ☐

Waterproof ☐

Animal proof ☐

Sunproof ☐

Fire Started ☐

Food Inventory

Rations ☐

Water ☐

Hunting ☐

Fishing ☐

Foraging ☐

Journey

Distance Covered

Trail Markers Used

Landmarks Sighted

Animal Prints

Map Sketch

Lat. Long.

Party Member	Status	Injuries	Treatment

Date

Conditions

Weather

Terrain

Shelter

Shelter Constructed ☐

Type of Shelter

Clothing/Coverings ☐

Waterproof ☐

Animal proof ☐

Sunproof ☐

Fire Started ☐

Food Inventory

Rations ☐

Water ☐

Hunting ☐

Fishing ☐

Foraging ☐

Journey

Distance Covered

Trail Markers Used

Landmarks Sighted

Animal Prints

Map Sketch

Lat.

Long.

Party Member	Status	Injuries	Treatment

Date

Conditions

Weather

Terrain

Food Inventory

Rations ☐

Water ☐

Hunting ☐

Fishing ☐

Foraging ☐

Journey

Distance Covered

Trail Markers Used

Landmarks Sighted

Animal Prints

Shelter

Shelter Constructed ☐

Type of Shelter

Clothing/Coverings ☐

Waterproof ☐

Animal proof ☐

Sunproof ☐

Fire Started ☐

Map Sketch

Lat. Long.

Party Member	Status	Injuries	Treatment

Date

Conditions

Weather

Terrain

Shelter

Shelter Constructed ☐

Type of Shelter

Clothing/Coverings ☐

Waterproof ☐

Animal proof ☐

Sunproof ☐

Fire Started ☐

Food Inventory

Rations ☐

Water ☐

Hunting ☐

Fishing ☐

Foraging ☐

Journey

Distance Covered

Trail Markers Used

Landmarks Sighted

Animal Prints

Map Sketch

Lat. Long.

Party Member	Status	Injuries	Treatment

Date ____________

Conditions

Weather

Terrain

Shelter

Shelter Constructed ☐

Type of Shelter

Clothing/Coverings ☐

Waterproof ☐

Animal proof ☐

Sunproof ☐

Fire Started ☐

Food Inventory

Rations ☐

Water ☐

Hunting ☐

Fishing ☐

Foraging ☐

Journey

Distance Covered

Trail Markers Used

Landmarks Sighted

Animal Prints

Map Sketch

Lat.

Long.

Party Member	Status	Injuries	Treatment

Date ____________

Conditions

Weather

Terrain

Food Inventory

Rations ☐

Water ☐

Hunting ☐

Fishing ☐

Foraging ☐

Journey

Distance Covered

Trail Markers Used

Landmarks Sighted

Animal Prints

Shelter

Shelter Constructed ☐

Type of Shelter

Clothing/Coverings ☐

Waterproof ☐

Animal proof ☐

Sunproof ☐

Fire Started ☐

Map Sketch

Lat. Long.

Party Member	Status	Injuries	Treatment

Date ______________

Conditions

Weather

Terrain

Shelter

Shelter Constructed ☐

Type of Shelter

____

____

____

Clothing/Coverings ☐

Waterproof ☐

Animal proof ☐

Sunproof ☐

Fire Started ☐

Food Inventory

Rations ☐

____

____

____

____

Water ☐

Hunting ☐

____

____

____

Fishing ☐

____

____

____

Foraging ☐

____

____

____

Journey

Distance Covered

Trail Markers Used

Landmarks Sighted

Animal Prints

Map Sketch

Lat. Long.

Party Member	Status	Injuries	Treatment

Date

Conditions

Weather

Terrain

Food Inventory

Rations ☐

Water ☐

Hunting ☐

Fishing ☐

Foraging ☐

Journey

Distance Covered

Trail Markers Used

Landmarks Sighted

Animal Prints

Shelter

Shelter Constructed ☐

Type of Shelter

Clothing/Coverings ☐

Waterproof ☐

Animal proof ☐

Sunproof ☐

Fire Started ☐

Map Sketch

Lat. Long.

Party Member	Status	Injuries	Treatment

Date ____________

Conditions

Weather

Terrain

Shelter

Shelter Constructed ☐

Type of Shelter

Clothing/Coverings ☐

Waterproof ☐

Animal proof ☐

Sunproof ☐

Fire Started ☐

Food Inventory

Rations ☐

Water ☐

Hunting ☐

Fishing ☐

Foraging ☐

Journey

Distance Covered

Trail Markers Used

Landmarks Sighted

Animal Prints

Map Sketch

Lat.

Long.

Party Member	Status	Injuries	Treatment

Date ______________

Conditions

Weather

Terrain

Shelter

Shelter Constructed ☐

Type of Shelter

Clothing/Coverings ☐

Waterproof ☐

Animal proof ☐

Sunproof ☐

Fire Started ☐

Food Inventory

Rations ☐

Water ☐

Hunting ☐

Fishing ☐

Foraging ☐

Journey

Distance Covered

Trail Markers Used

Landmarks Sighted

Animal Prints

Map Sketch

Lat. Long.

Party Member	Status	Injuries	Treatment

Date

Conditions

Weather

Terrain

Shelter

Shelter Constructed ☐

Type of Shelter

Clothing/Coverings ☐

Waterproof ☐

Animal proof ☐

Sunproof ☐

Fire Started ☐

Food Inventory

Rations ☐

Water ☐

Hunting ☐

Fishing ☐

Foraging ☐

Journey

Distance Covered

Trail Markers Used

Landmarks Sighted

Animal Prints

Map Sketch

Lat. Long.

Party Member	Status	Injuries	Treatment

Date

Conditions

Weather

Terrain

Food Inventory

Rations ☐

Water ☐

Hunting ☐

Fishing ☐

Foraging ☐

Journey

Distance Covered

Trail Markers Used

Landmarks Sighted

Animal Prints

Shelter

Shelter Constructed ☐

Type of Shelter

Clothing/Coverings ☐

Waterproof ☐

Animal proof ☐

Sunproof ☐

Fire Started ☐

Map Sketch

Lat. Long.

Party Member	Status	Injuries	Treatment

Date

Conditions

Weather

Terrain

Shelter

Shelter Constructed ☐

Type of Shelter

Clothing/Coverings ☐

Waterproof ☐

Animal proof ☐

Sunproof ☐

Fire Started ☐

Food Inventory

Rations ☐

Water ☐

Hunting ☐

Fishing ☐

Foraging ☐

Journey

Distance Covered

Trail Markers Used

Landmarks Sighted

Animal Prints

Map Sketch

Lat. Long.

Party Member	Status	Injuries	Treatment

Date

Conditions

Weather

Terrain

Shelter

Shelter Constructed ☐

Type of Shelter

Clothing/Coverings ☐

Waterproof ☐

Animal proof ☐

Sunproof ☐

Fire Started ☐

Food Inventory

Rations ☐

Water ☐

Hunting ☐

Fishing ☐

Foraging ☐

Journey

Distance Covered

Trail Markers Used

Landmarks Sighted

Animal Prints

Map Sketch

Lat. Long.

Party Member	Status	Injuries	Treatment

Date

Conditions

Weather

Terrain

Food Inventory

Rations ☐

Water ☐

Hunting ☐

Fishing ☐

Foraging ☐

Journey

Distance Covered

Trail Markers Used

Landmarks Sighted

Animal Prints

Shelter

Shelter Constructed ☐

Type of Shelter

Clothing/Coverings ☐

Waterproof ☐

Animal proof ☐

Sunproof ☐

Fire Started ☐

Map Sketch

Lat. Long.

Party Member	Status	Injuries	Treatment

Date

Conditions

Weather

Terrain

Shelter

Shelter Constructed ☐

Type of Shelter

Clothing/Coverings ☐

Waterproof ☐

Animal proof ☐

Sunproof ☐

Fire Started ☐

Food Inventory

Rations ☐

Water ☐

Hunting ☐

Fishing ☐

Foraging ☐

Journey

Distance Covered

Trail Markers Used

Landmarks Sighted

Animal Prints

Map Sketch

Lat. Long.

Party Member	Status	Injuries	Treatment

Date

Conditions

Weather

Terrain

Shelter

Shelter Constructed ☐

Type of Shelter

Clothing/Coverings ☐

Waterproof ☐

Animal proof ☐

Sunproof ☐

Fire Started ☐

Food Inventory

Rations ☐

Water ☐

Hunting ☐

Fishing ☐

Foraging ☐

Journey

Distance Covered

Trail Markers Used

Landmarks Sighted

Animal Prints

Map Sketch

Lat. Long.

Party Member	Status	Injuries	Treatment

Date

Conditions

Weather

Terrain

Shelter

Shelter Constructed ☐

Type of Shelter

Clothing/Coverings ☐

Waterproof ☐

Animal proof ☐

Sunproof ☐

Fire Started ☐

Food Inventory

Rations ☐

Water ☐

Hunting ☐

Fishing ☐

Foraging ☐

Journey

Distance Covered

Trail Markers Used

Landmarks Sighted

Animal Prints

Map Sketch

Lat.

Long.

Party Member	Status	Injuries	Treatment

Date

Conditions

Weather

Terrain

Shelter

Shelter Constructed ☐

Type of Shelter

Clothing/Coverings ☐

Waterproof ☐

Animal proof ☐

Sunproof ☐

Fire Started ☐

Food Inventory

Rations ☐

Water ☐

Hunting ☐

Fishing ☐

Foraging ☐

Journey

Distance Covered

Trail Markers Used

Landmarks Sighted

Animal Prints

Map Sketch

Lat. Long.

Party Member	Status	Injuries	Treatment

Date ____________

Conditions

Weather

Terrain

Shelter

Shelter Constructed ☐

Type of Shelter

Clothing/Coverings ☐

Waterproof ☐

Animal proof ☐

Sunproof ☐

Fire Started ☐

Food Inventory

Rations ☐

Water ☐

Hunting ☐

Fishing ☐

Foraging ☐

Journey

Distance Covered

Trail Markers Used

Landmarks Sighted

Animal Prints

Map Sketch

Lat.

Long.

Party Member	Status	Injuries	Treatment

Date

Conditions

Weather

Terrain

Shelter

Shelter Constructed ☐

Type of Shelter

Clothing/Coverings ☐

Waterproof ☐

Animal proof ☐

Sunproof ☐

Fire Started ☐

Food Inventory

Rations ☐

Water ☐

Hunting ☐

Fishing ☐

Foraging ☐

Journey

Distance Covered

Trail Markers Used

Landmarks Sighted

Animal Prints

Map Sketch

Lat.

Long.

Party Member	Status	Injuries	Treatment

Date

Conditions

Weather

Terrain

Food Inventory

Rations ☐

Water ☐

Hunting ☐

Fishing ☐

Foraging ☐

Journey

Distance Covered

Trail Markers Used

Landmarks Sighted

Animal Prints

Shelter

Shelter Constructed ☐

Type of Shelter

Clothing/Coverings ☐

Waterproof ☐

Animal proof ☐

Sunproof ☐

Fire Started ☐

Map Sketch

Lat. Long.

Party Member	Status	Injuries	Treatment

Date

Conditions

Weather

Terrain

Shelter

Shelter Constructed ☐

Type of Shelter

Clothing/Coverings ☐

Waterproof ☐

Animal proof ☐

Sunproof ☐

Fire Started ☐

Food Inventory

Rations ☐

Water ☐

Hunting ☐

Fishing ☐

Foraging ☐

Journey

Distance Covered

Trail Markers Used

Landmarks Sighted

Animal Prints

Map Sketch

Lat. Long.

Party Member	Status	Injuries	Treatment

Date ____________

Conditions

Weather

Terrain

Food Inventory

Rations ☐

Water ☐

Hunting ☐

Fishing ☐

Foraging ☐

Journey

Distance Covered

Trail Markers Used

Landmarks Sighted

Animal Prints

Shelter

Shelter Constructed ☐

Type of Shelter

Clothing/Coverings ☐

Waterproof ☐

Animal proof ☐

Sunproof ☐

Fire Started ☐

Map Sketch

Lat. Long.

Party Member	Status	Injuries	Treatment

Date

Conditions

Weather

Terrain

Shelter

Shelter Constructed ☐

Type of Shelter

Clothing/Coverings ☐

Waterproof ☐

Animal proof ☐

Sunproof ☐

Fire Started ☐

Food Inventory

Rations ☐

Water ☐

Hunting ☐

Fishing ☐

Foraging ☐

Journey

Distance Covered

Trail Markers Used

Landmarks Sighted

Animal Prints

Map Sketch

Lat. Long.

Party Member	Status	Injuries	Treatment

Date ____________

Conditions

Weather

Terrain

Shelter

Shelter Constructed ☐

Type of Shelter

Clothing/Coverings ☐

Waterproof ☐

Animal proof ☐

Sunproof ☐

Fire Started ☐

Food Inventory

Rations ☐

Water ☐

Hunting ☐

Fishing ☐

Foraging ☐

Journey

Distance Covered

Trail Markers Used

Landmarks Sighted

Animal Prints

Map Sketch

Lat. Long.

Party Member	Status	Injuries	Treatment

Date ____________

Conditions

Weather

Terrain

Food Inventory

Rations ☐

Water ☐

Hunting ☐

Fishing ☐

Foraging ☐

Journey

Distance Covered

Trail Markers Used

Landmarks Sighted

Animal Prints

Shelter

Shelter Constructed ☐

Type of Shelter

Clothing/Coverings ☐

Waterproof ☐

Animal proof ☐

Sunproof ☐

Fire Started ☐

Map Sketch

Lat. Long.

Party Member	Status	Injuries	Treatment

Date

Conditions

Weather

Terrain

Shelter

Shelter Constructed ☐

Type of Shelter

Clothing/Coverings ☐

Waterproof ☐

Animal proof ☐

Sunproof ☐

Fire Started ☐

Food Inventory

Rations ☐

Water ☐

Hunting ☐

Fishing ☐

Foraging ☐

Journey

Distance Covered

Trail Markers Used

Landmarks Sighted

Animal Prints

Map Sketch

Lat. Long.

Party Member	Status	Injuries	Treatment

Date

Conditions

Weather

Terrain

Shelter

Shelter Constructed ☐

Type of Shelter

Clothing/Coverings ☐

Waterproof ☐

Animal proof ☐

Sunproof ☐

Fire Started ☐

Food Inventory

Rations ☐

Water ☐

Hunting ☐

Fishing ☐

Foraging ☐

Journey

Distance Covered

Trail Markers Used

Landmarks Sighted

Animal Prints

Map Sketch

Lat.

Long.

Party Member	Status	Injuries	Treatment

Date

Conditions

Weather

Terrain

Food Inventory

Rations ☐

Water ☐

Hunting ☐

Fishing ☐

Foraging ☐

Journey

Distance Covered

Trail Markers Used

Landmarks Sighted

Animal Prints

Shelter

Shelter Constructed ☐

Type of Shelter

Clothing/Coverings ☐

Waterproof ☐

Animal proof ☐

Sunproof ☐

Fire Started ☐

Map Sketch

Lat. Long.

Party Member	Status	Injuries	Treatment

Date

Conditions

Weather

Terrain

Shelter

Shelter Constructed ☐

Type of Shelter

Clothing/Coverings ☐

Waterproof ☐

Animal proof ☐

Sunproof ☐

Fire Started ☐

Food Inventory

Rations ☐

Water ☐

Hunting ☐

Fishing ☐

Foraging ☐

Journey

Distance Covered

Trail Markers Used

Landmarks Sighted

Animal Prints

Map Sketch

Lat. Long.

Party Member	Status	Injuries	Treatment

Date ____________

Conditions

Weather

Terrain

Food Inventory

Rations ☐

Water ☐

Hunting ☐

Fishing ☐

Foraging ☐

Journey

Distance Covered

Trail Markers Used

Landmarks Sighted

Animal Prints

Shelter

Shelter Constructed ☐

Type of Shelter

Clothing/Coverings ☐

Waterproof ☐

Animal proof ☐

Sunproof ☐

Fire Started ☐

Map Sketch

Lat. Long.

Party Member	Status	Injuries	Treatment

Date

Conditions

Weather

Terrain

Shelter

Shelter Constructed ☐

Type of Shelter

Clothing/Coverings ☐

Waterproof ☐

Animal proof ☐

Sunproof ☐

Fire Started ☐

Food Inventory

Rations ☐

Water ☐

Hunting ☐

Fishing ☐

Foraging ☐

Journey

Distance Covered

Trail Markers Used

Landmarks Sighted

Animal Prints

Map Sketch

Lat. Long.

Party Member	Status	Injuries	Treatment

Date ______

Conditions

Weather

Terrain

Food Inventory

Rations ☐

Water ☐

Hunting ☐

Fishing ☐

Foraging ☐

Journey

Distance Covered

Trail Markers Used

Landmarks Sighted

Animal Prints

Shelter

Shelter Constructed ☐

Type of Shelter

Clothing/Coverings ☐

Waterproof ☐

Animal proof ☐

Sunproof ☐

Fire Started ☐

Map Sketch

Lat. Long.

Party Member	Status	Injuries	Treatment

Date ____________

Conditions

Weather

Terrain

Shelter

Shelter Constructed ☐

Type of Shelter

____

____

____

Clothing/Coverings ☐

Waterproof ☐

Animal proof ☐

Sunproof ☐

Fire Started ☐

Food Inventory

Rations ☐

____

____

____

____

Water ☐

Hunting ☐

____

____

____

Fishing ☐

____

____

____

Foraging ☐

____

____

____

Journey

Distance Covered

Trail Markers Used

Landmarks Sighted

Animal Prints

Map Sketch

Lat. Long.

Party Member	Status	Injuries	Treatment

Date ______

Conditions

Weather

Terrain

Food Inventory

Rations ☐

Water ☐

Hunting ☐

Fishing ☐

Foraging ☐

Journey

Distance Covered

Trail Markers Used

Landmarks Sighted

Animal Prints

Shelter

Shelter Constructed ☐

Type of Shelter

Clothing/Coverings ☐

Waterproof ☐

Animal proof ☐

Sunproof ☐

Fire Started ☐

Map Sketch

Lat. Long.

Party Member	Status	Injuries	Treatment

Date ______

Conditions

Weather

Terrain

Food Inventory

Rations ☐

Water ☐

Hunting ☐

Fishing ☐

Foraging ☐

Journey

Distance Covered

Trail Markers Used

Landmarks Sighted

Animal Prints

Shelter

Shelter Constructed ☐

Type of Shelter

Clothing/Coverings ☐

Waterproof ☐

Animal proof ☐

Sunproof ☐

Fire Started ☐

Map Sketch

Lat. Long.

Party Member	Status	Injuries	Treatment

Date ______

Conditions

Weather

Terrain

Food Inventory

Rations ☐

Water ☐

Hunting ☐

Fishing ☐

Foraging ☐

Journey

Distance Covered

Trail Markers Used

Landmarks Sighted

Animal Prints

Shelter

Shelter Constructed ☐

Type of Shelter

Clothing/Coverings ☐

Waterproof ☐

Animal proof ☐

Sunproof ☐

Fire Started ☐

Map Sketch

Lat. Long.

Party Member	Status	Injuries	Treatment

Date

Conditions

Weather

Terrain

Shelter

Shelter Constructed ☐

Type of Shelter

Clothing/Coverings ☐

Waterproof ☐

Animal proof ☐

Sunproof ☐

Fire Started ☐

Food Inventory

Rations ☐

Water ☐

Hunting ☐

Fishing ☐

Foraging ☐

Journey

Distance Covered

Trail Markers Used

Landmarks Sighted

Animal Prints

Map Sketch

Lat.

Long.

Party Member	Status	Injuries	Treatment

Date ____________

Conditions

Weather

Terrain

Food Inventory

Rations ☐

Water ☐

Hunting ☐

Fishing ☐

Foraging ☐

Journey

Distance Covered

Trail Markers Used

Landmarks Sighted

Animal Prints

Shelter

Shelter Constructed ☐

Type of Shelter

Clothing/Coverings ☐

Waterproof ☐

Animal proof ☐

Sunproof ☐

Fire Started ☐

Map Sketch

Lat. Long.

Party Member	Status	Injuries	Treatment

Date

Conditions

Weather

Terrain

Shelter

Shelter Constructed ☐

Type of Shelter

Clothing/Coverings ☐

Waterproof ☐

Animal proof ☐

Sunproof ☐

Fire Started ☐

Food Inventory

Rations ☐

Water ☐

Hunting ☐

Fishing ☐

Foraging ☐

Journey

Distance Covered

Trail Markers Used

Landmarks Sighted

Animal Prints

Map Sketch

Lat.

Long.

Party Member	Status	Injuries	Treatment

Date

Conditions

Weather

Terrain

Shelter

Shelter Constructed ☐

Type of Shelter

Clothing/Coverings ☐

Waterproof ☐

Animal proof ☐

Sunproof ☐

Fire Started ☐

Food Inventory

Rations ☐

Water ☐

Hunting ☐

Fishing ☐

Foraging ☐

Journey

Distance Covered

Trail Markers Used

Landmarks Sighted

Animal Prints

Map Sketch

Lat. Long.

Party Member	Status	Injuries	Treatment

Date

Conditions

Weather

Terrain

Food Inventory

Rations ☐

Water ☐

Hunting ☐

Fishing ☐

Foraging ☐

Journey

Distance Covered

Trail Markers Used

Landmarks Sighted

Animal Prints

Shelter

Shelter Constructed ☐

Type of Shelter

Clothing/Coverings ☐

Waterproof ☐

Animal proof ☐

Sunproof ☐

Fire Started ☐

Map Sketch

Lat. Long.

Party Member	Status	Injuries	Treatment

Date

Conditions

Weather

Terrain

Shelter

Shelter Constructed ☐

Type of Shelter

Clothing/Coverings ☐

Waterproof ☐

Animal proof ☐

Sunproof ☐

Fire Started ☐

Food Inventory

Rations ☐

Water ☐

Hunting ☐

Fishing ☐

Foraging ☐

Journey

Distance Covered

Trail Markers Used

Landmarks Sighted

Animal Prints

Map Sketch

Lat.

Long.

Party Member	Status	Injuries	Treatment

Date ____________

Conditions

Weather

Terrain

Shelter

Shelter Constructed ☐

Type of Shelter

Clothing/Coverings ☐

Waterproof ☐

Animal proof ☐

Sunproof ☐

Fire Started ☐

Food Inventory

Rations ☐

Water ☐

Hunting ☐

Fishing ☐

Foraging ☐

Journey

Distance Covered

Trail Markers Used

Landmarks Sighted

Animal Prints

Map Sketch

Lat. Long.

Party Member	Status	Injuries	Treatment

Date ______

Conditions

Weather

Terrain

Shelter

Shelter Constructed ☐

Type of Shelter

Clothing/Coverings ☐

Waterproof ☐

Animal proof ☐

Sunproof ☐

Fire Started ☐

Food Inventory

Rations ☐

Water ☐

Hunting ☐

Fishing ☐

Foraging ☐

Journey

Distance Covered

Trail Markers Used

Landmarks Sighted

Animal Prints

Map Sketch

Lat.

Long.

Party Member	Status	Injuries	Treatment

Date ____________

Conditions

Weather

Terrain

Food Inventory

Rations ☐

Water ☐

Hunting ☐

Fishing ☐

Foraging ☐

Journey

Distance Covered

Trail Markers Used

Landmarks Sighted

Animal Prints

Shelter

Shelter Constructed ☐

Type of Shelter

Clothing/Coverings ☐

Waterproof ☐

Animal proof ☐

Sunproof ☐

Fire Started ☐

Map Sketch

Lat. Long.

Party Member	Status	Injuries	Treatment

Date

Conditions

Weather

Terrain

Food Inventory

Rations ☐

Water ☐

Hunting ☐

Fishing ☐

Foraging ☐

Journey

Distance Covered

Trail Markers Used

Landmarks Sighted

Animal Prints

Shelter

Shelter Constructed ☐

Type of Shelter

Clothing/Coverings ☐

Waterproof ☐

Animal proof ☐

Sunproof ☐

Fire Started ☐

Map Sketch

Lat.

Long.

Party Member	Status	Injuries	Treatment

Date

Conditions

Weather

Terrain

Shelter

Shelter Constructed ☐

Type of Shelter

Clothing/Coverings ☐

Waterproof ☐

Animal proof ☐

Sunproof ☐

Fire Started ☐

Food Inventory

Rations ☐

Water ☐

Hunting ☐

Fishing ☐

Foraging ☐

Journey

Distance Covered

Trail Markers Used

Landmarks Sighted

Animal Prints

Map Sketch

Lat.

Long.

Party Member	Status	Injuries	Treatment

Date ____________

Conditions

Weather

Terrain

Shelter

Shelter Constructed ☐

Type of Shelter

Clothing/Coverings ☐

Waterproof ☐

Animal proof ☐

Sunproof ☐

Fire Started ☐

Food Inventory

Rations ☐

Water ☐

Hunting ☐

Fishing ☐

Foraging ☐

Journey

Distance Covered

Trail Markers Used

Landmarks Sighted

Animal Prints

Map Sketch

Lat.

Long.

Party Member	Status	Injuries	Treatment

Date ____________

Conditions

Weather

Terrain

Food Inventory

Rations ☐

Water ☐

Hunting ☐

Fishing ☐

Foraging ☐

Journey

Distance Covered

Trail Markers Used

Landmarks Sighted

Animal Prints

Shelter

Shelter Constructed ☐

Type of Shelter

Clothing/Coverings ☐

Waterproof ☐

Animal proof ☐

Sunproof ☐

Fire Started ☐

Map Sketch

Lat. Long.

Party Member	Status	Injuries	Treatment

Date ______________

Conditions

Weather

Terrain

Shelter

Shelter Constructed ☐

Type of Shelter

Clothing/Coverings ☐

Waterproof ☐

Animal proof ☐

Sunproof ☐

Fire Started ☐

Food Inventory

Rations ☐

Water ☐

Hunting ☐

Fishing ☐

Foraging ☐

Journey

Distance Covered

Trail Markers Used

Landmarks Sighted

Animal Prints

Map Sketch

Lat. Long.

Party Member	Status	Injuries	Treatment

Date

Conditions

Weather

Terrain

Food Inventory

Rations ☐

Water ☐

Hunting ☐

Fishing ☐

Foraging ☐

Journey

Distance Covered

Trail Markers Used

Landmarks Sighted

Animal Prints

Shelter

Shelter Constructed ☐

Type of Shelter

Clothing/Coverings ☐

Waterproof ☐

Animal proof ☐

Sunproof ☐

Fire Started ☐

Map Sketch

Lat. Long.

Party Member	Status	Injuries	Treatment

Date

Conditions

Weather

Terrain

Shelter

Shelter Constructed ☐

Type of Shelter

Clothing/Coverings ☐

Waterproof ☐

Animal proof ☐

Sunproof ☐

Fire Started ☐

Food Inventory

Rations ☐

Water ☐

Hunting ☐

Fishing ☐

Foraging ☐

Journey

Distance Covered

Trail Markers Used

Landmarks Sighted

Animal Prints

Map Sketch

Lat.

Long.

Party Member	Status	Injuries	Treatment

Date

Conditions

Weather

Terrain

Food Inventory

Rations ☐

Water ☐

Hunting ☐

Fishing ☐

Foraging ☐

Journey

Distance Covered

Trail Markers Used

Landmarks Sighted

Animal Prints

Shelter

Shelter Constructed ☐

Type of Shelter

Clothing/Coverings ☐

Waterproof ☐

Animal proof ☐

Sunproof ☐

Fire Started ☐

Map Sketch

Lat.

Long.

Party Member	Status	Injuries	Treatment

Date

Conditions

Weather

Terrain

Food Inventory

Rations ☐

Water ☐

Hunting ☐

Fishing ☐

Foraging ☐

Journey

Distance Covered

Trail Markers Used

Landmarks Sighted

Animal Prints

Shelter

Shelter Constructed ☐

Type of Shelter

Clothing/Coverings ☐

Waterproof ☐

Animal proof ☐

Sunproof ☐

Fire Started ☐

Map Sketch

Lat. Long.

Party Member	Status	Injuries	Treatment

Date

Conditions

Weather

Terrain

Shelter

Shelter Constructed ☐

Type of Shelter

Clothing/Coverings ☐

Waterproof ☐

Animal proof ☐

Sunproof ☐

Fire Started ☐

Food Inventory

Rations ☐

Water ☐

Hunting ☐

Fishing ☐

Foraging ☐

Journey

Distance Covered

Trail Markers Used

Landmarks Sighted

Animal Prints

Map Sketch

Lat. Long.

Party Member	Status	Injuries	Treatment

Date

Conditions

Weather

Terrain

Food Inventory

Rations ☐

Water ☐

Hunting ☐

Fishing ☐

Foraging ☐

Journey

Distance Covered

Trail Markers Used

Landmarks Sighted

Animal Prints

Shelter

Shelter Constructed ☐

Type of Shelter

Clothing/Coverings ☐

Waterproof ☐

Animal proof ☐

Sunproof ☐

Fire Started ☐

Map Sketch

Lat. Long.

Party Member	Status	Injuries	Treatment

Date ____________

Conditions

Weather

Terrain

Food Inventory

Rations ☐

Water ☐

Hunting ☐

Fishing ☐

Foraging ☐

Journey

Distance Covered

Trail Markers Used

Landmarks Sighted

Animal Prints

Shelter

Shelter Constructed ☐

Type of Shelter

Clothing/Coverings ☐

Waterproof ☐

Animal proof ☐

Sunproof ☐

Fire Started ☐

Map Sketch

Lat. Long.

Party Member	Status	Injuries	Treatment

Date ____________

Conditions

Weather

Terrain

Shelter

Shelter Constructed ☐

Type of Shelter

Clothing/Coverings ☐

Waterproof ☐

Animal proof ☐

Sunproof ☐

Fire Started ☐

Food Inventory

Rations ☐

Water ☐

Hunting ☐

Fishing ☐

Foraging ☐

Journey

Distance Covered

Trail Markers Used

Landmarks Sighted

Animal Prints

Map Sketch

Lat. Long.

Party Member	Status	Injuries	Treatment

Date

Conditions

Weather

Terrain

Shelter

Shelter Constructed ☐

Type of Shelter

Clothing/Coverings ☐

Waterproof ☐

Animal proof ☐

Sunproof ☐

Fire Started ☐

Food Inventory

Rations ☐

Water ☐

Hunting ☐

Fishing ☐

Foraging ☐

Journey

Distance Covered

Trail Markers Used

Landmarks Sighted

Animal Prints

Map Sketch

Lat. Long.

Party Member	Status	Injuries	Treatment

Date

Conditions

Weather

Terrain

Shelter

Shelter Constructed ☐

Type of Shelter

Clothing/Coverings ☐

Waterproof ☐

Animal proof ☐

Sunproof ☐

Fire Started ☐

Food Inventory

Rations ☐

Water ☐

Hunting ☐

Fishing ☐

Foraging ☐

Journey

Distance Covered

Trail Markers Used

Landmarks Sighted

Animal Prints

Map Sketch

Lat. Long.

Party Member	Status	Injuries	Treatment

Date

Conditions

Weather

Terrain

Food Inventory

Rations ☐

Water ☐

Hunting ☐

Fishing ☐

Foraging ☐

Journey

Distance Covered

Trail Markers Used

Landmarks Sighted

Animal Prints

Shelter

Shelter Constructed ☐

Type of Shelter

Clothing/Coverings ☐

Waterproof ☐

Animal proof ☐

Sunproof ☐

Fire Started ☐

Map Sketch

Lat. Long.

Party Member	Status	Injuries	Treatment

Date

Conditions

Weather

Terrain

Shelter

Shelter Constructed ☐

Type of Shelter

Clothing/Coverings ☐

Waterproof ☐

Animal proof ☐

Sunproof ☐

Fire Started ☐

Food Inventory

Rations ☐

Water ☐

Hunting ☐

Fishing ☐

Foraging ☐

Journey

Distance Covered

Trail Markers Used

Landmarks Sighted

Animal Prints

Map Sketch

Lat. Long.

Party Member	Status	Injuries	Treatment

Date ______________

Conditions

Weather

Terrain

Food Inventory

Rations ☐

Water ☐

Hunting ☐

Fishing ☐

Foraging ☐

Journey

Distance Covered

Trail Markers Used

Landmarks Sighted

Animal Prints

Shelter

Shelter Constructed ☐

Type of Shelter

Clothing/Coverings ☐

Waterproof ☐

Animal proof ☐

Sunproof ☐

Fire Started ☐

Map Sketch

Lat. Long.

Party Member	Status	Injuries	Treatment

Date

Conditions

Weather

Terrain

Shelter

Shelter Constructed ☐

Type of Shelter

Clothing/Coverings ☐

Waterproof ☐

Animal proof ☐

Sunproof ☐

Fire Started ☐

Food Inventory

Rations ☐

Water ☐

Hunting ☐

Fishing ☐

Foraging ☐

Journey

Distance Covered

Trail Markers Used

Landmarks Sighted

Animal Prints

Map Sketch

Lat. Long.

Party Member	Status	Injuries	Treatment

Date ____________

Conditions

Weather

Terrain

Shelter

Shelter Constructed ☐

Type of Shelter

Clothing/Coverings ☐

Waterproof ☐

Animal proof ☐

Sunproof ☐

Fire Started ☐

Food Inventory

Rations ☐

Water ☐

Hunting ☐

Fishing ☐

Foraging ☐

Journey

Distance Covered

Trail Markers Used

Landmarks Sighted

Animal Prints

Map Sketch

Lat. Long.

Party Member	Status	Injuries	Treatment

Date ____________

Conditions

Weather

Terrain

Food Inventory

Rations ☐

Water ☐

Hunting ☐

Fishing ☐

Foraging ☐

Journey

Distance Covered

Trail Markers Used

Landmarks Sighted

Animal Prints

Shelter

Shelter Constructed ☐

Type of Shelter

Clothing/Coverings ☐

Waterproof ☐

Animal proof ☐

Sunproof ☐

Fire Started ☐

Map Sketch

Lat. Long.

Party Member	Status	Injuries	Treatment

Date

Conditions

Weather

Terrain

Shelter

Shelter Constructed ☐

Type of Shelter

Clothing/Coverings ☐

Waterproof ☐

Animal proof ☐

Sunproof ☐

Fire Started ☐

Food Inventory

Rations ☐

Water ☐

Hunting ☐

Fishing ☐

Foraging ☐

Journey

Distance Covered

Trail Markers Used

Landmarks Sighted

Animal Prints

Map Sketch

Lat. Long.

Party Member	Status	Injuries	Treatment

Date

Conditions

Weather

Terrain

Shelter

Shelter Constructed ☐

Type of Shelter

Clothing/Coverings ☐

Waterproof ☐

Animal proof ☐

Sunproof ☐

Fire Started ☐

Food Inventory

Rations ☐

Water ☐

Hunting ☐

Fishing ☐

Foraging ☐

Journey

Distance Covered

Trail Markers Used

Landmarks Sighted

Animal Prints

Map Sketch

Lat. Long.

Party Member	Status	Injuries	Treatment

Date ____________

Conditions

Weather

Terrain

Shelter

Shelter Constructed ☐

Type of Shelter

Clothing/Coverings ☐

Waterproof ☐

Animal proof ☐

Sunproof ☐

Fire Started ☐

Food Inventory

Rations ☐

Water ☐

Hunting ☐

Fishing ☐

Foraging ☐

Journey

Distance Covered

Trail Markers Used

Landmarks Sighted

Animal Prints

Map Sketch

Lat. Long.

Party Member	Status	Injuries	Treatment

Date ______________

Conditions

Weather

Terrain

Shelter

Shelter Constructed ☐

Type of Shelter

Clothing/Coverings ☐

Waterproof ☐

Animal proof ☐

Sunproof ☐

Fire Started ☐

Food Inventory

Rations ☐

Water ☐

Hunting ☐

Fishing ☐

Foraging ☐

Journey

Distance Covered

Trail Markers Used

Landmarks Sighted

Animal Prints

Map Sketch

Lat.

Long.

Party Member	Status	Injuries	Treatment

Date ____________

Conditions

Weather

Terrain

Food Inventory

Rations ☐

Water ☐

Hunting ☐

Fishing ☐

Foraging ☐

Journey

Distance Covered

Trail Markers Used

Landmarks Sighted

Animal Prints

Shelter

Shelter Constructed ☐

Type of Shelter

Clothing/Coverings ☐

Waterproof ☐

Animal proof ☐

Sunproof ☐

Fire Started ☐

Map Sketch

Lat. Long.

Party Member	Status	Injuries	Treatment

Date ____________

Conditions

Weather

Terrain

Shelter

Shelter Constructed ☐

Type of Shelter

Clothing/Coverings ☐

Waterproof ☐

Animal proof ☐

Sunproof ☐

Fire Started ☐

Food Inventory

Rations ☐

Water ☐

Hunting ☐

Fishing ☐

Foraging ☐

Journey

Distance Covered

Trail Markers Used

Landmarks Sighted

Animal Prints

Map Sketch

Lat.

Long.

Party Member	Status	Injuries	Treatment

Date

Conditions

Weather

Terrain

Shelter

Shelter Constructed ☐

Type of Shelter

Clothing/Coverings ☐

Waterproof ☐

Animal proof ☐

Sunproof ☐

Fire Started ☐

Food Inventory

Rations ☐

Water ☐

Hunting ☐

Fishing ☐

Foraging ☐

Journey

Distance Covered

Trail Markers Used

Landmarks Sighted

Animal Prints

Map Sketch

Lat. Long.

Party Member	Status	Injuries	Treatment

Date

Conditions

Weather

Terrain

Shelter

Shelter Constructed ☐

Type of Shelter

Clothing/Coverings ☐

Waterproof ☐

Animal proof ☐

Sunproof ☐

Fire Started ☐

Food Inventory

Rations ☐

Water ☐

Hunting ☐

Fishing ☐

Foraging ☐

Journey

Distance Covered

Trail Markers Used

Landmarks Sighted

Animal Prints

Map Sketch

Lat.

Long.

Party Member	Status	Injuries	Treatment

Date

Conditions

Weather

Terrain

Shelter

Shelter Constructed ☐

Type of Shelter

Clothing/Coverings ☐

Waterproof ☐

Animal proof ☐

Sunproof ☐

Fire Started ☐

Food Inventory

Rations ☐

Water ☐

Hunting ☐

Fishing ☐

Foraging ☐

Journey

Distance Covered

Trail Markers Used

Landmarks Sighted

Animal Prints

Map Sketch

Lat. Long.

Party Member	Status	Injuries	Treatment

Date ____________

Conditions

Weather

Terrain

Shelter

Shelter Constructed ☐

Type of Shelter

Clothing/Coverings ☐

Waterproof ☐

Animal proof ☐

Sunproof ☐

Fire Started ☐

Food Inventory

Rations ☐

Water ☐

Hunting ☐

Fishing ☐

Foraging ☐

Journey

Distance Covered

Trail Markers Used

Landmarks Sighted

Animal Prints

Map Sketch

Lat.

Long.

Party Member	Status	Injuries	Treatment

Date ____________

Conditions

Weather

Terrain

Shelter

Shelter Constructed ☐

Type of Shelter

Clothing/Coverings ☐

Waterproof ☐

Animal proof ☐

Sunproof ☐

Fire Started ☐

Food Inventory

Rations ☐

Water ☐

Hunting ☐

Fishing ☐

Foraging ☐

Journey

Distance Covered

Trail Markers Used

Landmarks Sighted

Animal Prints

Map Sketch

Lat. Long.

Party Member	Status	Injuries	Treatment

Date ______

Conditions

Weather

Terrain

Shelter

Shelter Constructed ☐

Type of Shelter

Clothing/Coverings ☐

Waterproof ☐

Animal proof ☐

Sunproof ☐

Fire Started ☐

Food Inventory

Rations ☐

Water ☐

Hunting ☐

Fishing ☐

Foraging ☐

Journey

Distance Covered

Trail Markers Used

Landmarks Sighted

Animal Prints

Map Sketch

Lat.

Long.

Party Member	Status	Injuries	Treatment

Date ______

Conditions

Weather

Terrain

Food Inventory

Rations ☐

Water ☐

Hunting ☐

Fishing ☐

Foraging ☐

Journey

Distance Covered

Trail Markers Used

Landmarks Sighted

Animal Prints

Shelter

Shelter Constructed ☐

Type of Shelter

Clothing/Coverings ☐

Waterproof ☐

Animal proof ☐

Sunproof ☐

Fire Started ☐

Map Sketch

Lat. Long.

Party Member	Status	Injuries	Treatment

Date

Conditions

Weather

Terrain

Shelter

Shelter Constructed ☐

Type of Shelter

Clothing/Coverings ☐

Waterproof ☐

Animal proof ☐

Sunproof ☐

Fire Started ☐

Food Inventory

Rations ☐

Water ☐

Hunting ☐

Fishing ☐

Foraging ☐

Journey

Distance Covered

Trail Markers Used

Landmarks Sighted

Animal Prints

Map Sketch

Lat.

Long.

Party Member	Status	Injuries	Treatment

Date

Conditions

Weather

Terrain

Shelter

Shelter Constructed ☐

Type of Shelter

Clothing/Coverings ☐

Waterproof ☐

Animal proof ☐

Sunproof ☐

Fire Started ☐

Food Inventory

Rations ☐

Water ☐

Hunting ☐

Fishing ☐

Foraging ☐

Journey

Distance Covered

Trail Markers Used

Landmarks Sighted

Animal Prints

Map Sketch

Lat.

Long.

Party Member	Status	Injuries	Treatment

Date

Conditions

Weather

Terrain

Shelter

Shelter Constructed ☐

Type of Shelter

Clothing/Coverings ☐

Waterproof ☐

Animal proof ☐

Sunproof ☐

Fire Started ☐

Food Inventory

Rations ☐

Water ☐

Hunting ☐

Fishing ☐

Foraging ☐

Journey

Distance Covered

Trail Markers Used

Landmarks Sighted

Animal Prints

Map Sketch

Lat. Long.

Party Member	Status	Injuries	Treatment

Date ______

Conditions

Weather

Terrain

Shelter

Shelter Constructed ☐

Type of Shelter

Clothing/Coverings ☐

Waterproof ☐

Animal proof ☐

Sunproof ☐

Fire Started ☐

Food Inventory

Rations ☐

Water ☐

Hunting ☐

Fishing ☐

Foraging ☐

Journey

Distance Covered

Trail Markers Used

Landmarks Sighted

Animal Prints

Map Sketch

Lat. Long.

Party Member	Status	Injuries	Treatment

Date ____________

Conditions

Weather

Terrain

Shelter

Shelter Constructed ☐

Type of Shelter

____

____

____

Clothing/Coverings ☐

Waterproof ☐

Animal proof ☐

Sunproof ☐

Fire Started ☐

Food Inventory

Rations ☐

____

____

____

____

Water ☐

Hunting ☐

____

____

____

Fishing ☐

____

____

____

Foraging ☐

____

____

____

Journey

Distance Covered

Trail Markers Used

Landmarks Sighted

Animal Prints

Map Sketch

Lat. Long.

Party Member	Status	Injuries	Treatment

Date

Conditions

Weather

Terrain

Shelter

Shelter Constructed ☐

Type of Shelter

Clothing/Coverings ☐

Waterproof ☐

Animal proof ☐

Sunproof ☐

Fire Started ☐

Food Inventory

Rations ☐

Water ☐

Hunting ☐

Fishing ☐

Foraging ☐

Journey

Distance Covered

Trail Markers Used

Landmarks Sighted

Animal Prints

Map Sketch

Lat. Long.

Party Member	Status	Injuries	Treatment

Date

Conditions

Weather

Terrain

Shelter

Shelter Constructed ☐

Type of Shelter

Clothing/Coverings ☐

Waterproof ☐

Animal proof ☐

Sunproof ☐

Fire Started ☐

Food Inventory

Rations ☐

Water ☐

Hunting ☐

Fishing ☐

Foraging ☐

Journey

Distance Covered

Trail Markers Used

Landmarks Sighted

Animal Prints

Map Sketch

Lat. Long.

Party Member	Status	Injuries	Treatment

Date ______________

Conditions

Weather

Terrain

Shelter

Shelter Constructed ☐

Type of Shelter

Clothing/Coverings ☐

Waterproof ☐

Animal proof ☐

Sunproof ☐

Fire Started ☐

Food Inventory

Rations ☐

Water ☐

Hunting ☐

Fishing ☐

Foraging ☐

Journey

Distance Covered

Trail Markers Used

Landmarks Sighted

Animal Prints

Map Sketch

Lat. Long.

Party Member	Status	Injuries	Treatment

Date

Conditions

Weather

Terrain

Shelter

Shelter Constructed ☐

Type of Shelter

Clothing/Coverings ☐

Waterproof ☐

Animal proof ☐

Sunproof ☐

Fire Started ☐

Food Inventory

Rations ☐

Water ☐

Hunting ☐

Fishing ☐

Foraging ☐

Journey

Distance Covered

Trail Markers Used

Landmarks Sighted

Animal Prints

Map Sketch

Lat. Long.

Party Member	Status	Injuries	Treatment

Date

Conditions

Weather

Terrain

Food Inventory

Rations ☐

Water ☐

Hunting ☐

Fishing ☐

Foraging ☐

Journey

Distance Covered

Trail Markers Used

Landmarks Sighted

Animal Prints

Shelter

Shelter Constructed ☐

Type of Shelter

Clothing/Coverings ☐

Waterproof ☐

Animal proof ☐

Sunproof ☐

Fire Started ☐

Map Sketch

Lat. Long.

Party Member	Status	Injuries	Treatment

Date

Conditions

Weather

Terrain

Shelter

Shelter Constructed ☐

Type of Shelter

Clothing/Coverings ☐

Waterproof ☐

Animal proof ☐

Sunproof ☐

Fire Started ☐

Food Inventory

Rations ☐

Water ☐

Hunting ☐

Fishing ☐

Foraging ☐

Journey

Distance Covered

Trail Markers Used

Landmarks Sighted

Animal Prints

Map Sketch

Lat. Long.

Party Member	Status	Injuries	Treatment

Date ____________

Conditions

Weather

Terrain

Shelter

Shelter Constructed ☐

Type of Shelter

Clothing/Coverings ☐

Waterproof ☐

Animal proof ☐

Sunproof ☐

Fire Started ☐

Food Inventory

Rations ☐

Water ☐

Hunting ☐

Fishing ☐

Foraging ☐

Journey

Distance Covered

Trail Markers Used

Landmarks Sighted

Animal Prints

Map Sketch

Lat. Long.

Party Member	Status	Injuries	Treatment

Date

Conditions

Weather

Terrain

Shelter

Shelter Constructed ☐

Type of Shelter

Clothing/Coverings ☐

Waterproof ☐

Animal proof ☐

Sunproof ☐

Fire Started ☐

Food Inventory

Rations ☐

Water ☐

Hunting ☐

Fishing ☐

Foraging ☐

Journey

Distance Covered

Trail Markers Used

Landmarks Sighted

Animal Prints

Map Sketch

Lat.

Long.

Party Member	Status	Injuries	Treatment

Date

Conditions

Weather

Terrain

Shelter

Shelter Constructed ☐

Type of Shelter

Clothing/Coverings ☐

Waterproof ☐

Animal proof ☐

Sunproof ☐

Fire Started ☐

Food Inventory

Rations ☐

Water ☐

Hunting ☐

Fishing ☐

Foraging ☐

Journey

Distance Covered

Trail Markers Used

Landmarks Sighted

Animal Prints

Map Sketch

Lat. Long.

Party Member	Status	Injuries	Treatment

Date ______________

Conditions

Weather

Terrain

Shelter

Shelter Constructed ☐

Type of Shelter

Clothing/Coverings ☐

Waterproof ☐

Animal proof ☐

Sunproof ☐

Fire Started ☐

Food Inventory

Rations ☐

Water ☐

Hunting ☐

Fishing ☐

Foraging ☐

Journey

Distance Covered

Trail Markers Used

Landmarks Sighted

Animal Prints

Map Sketch

Lat.

Long.

Party Member	Status	Injuries	Treatment

Date

Conditions

Weather

Terrain

Shelter

Shelter Constructed ☐

Type of Shelter

Clothing/Coverings ☐

Waterproof ☐

Animal proof ☐

Sunproof ☐

Fire Started ☐

Food Inventory

Rations ☐

Water ☐

Hunting ☐

Fishing ☐

Foraging ☐

Journey

Distance Covered

Trail Markers Used

Landmarks Sighted

Animal Prints

Map Sketch

Lat. Long.

Party Member	Status	Injuries	Treatment

Date

Conditions

Weather

Terrain

Food Inventory

Rations ☐

Water ☐

Hunting ☐

Fishing ☐

Foraging ☐

Journey

Distance Covered

Trail Markers Used

Landmarks Sighted

Animal Prints

Shelter

Shelter Constructed ☐

Type of Shelter

Clothing/Coverings ☐

Waterproof ☐

Animal proof ☐

Sunproof ☐

Fire Started ☐

Map Sketch

Lat. Long.

Party Member	Status	Injuries	Treatment

Date

Conditions

Weather

Terrain

Shelter

Shelter Constructed ☐

Type of Shelter

Clothing/Coverings ☐

Waterproof ☐

Animal proof ☐

Sunproof ☐

Fire Started ☐

Food Inventory

Rations ☐

Water ☐

Hunting ☐

Fishing ☐

Foraging ☐

Journey

Distance Covered

Trail Markers Used

Landmarks Sighted

Animal Prints

Map Sketch

Lat. Long.

Party Member	Status	Injuries	Treatment

Date ____________

Conditions

Weather

Terrain

Shelter

Shelter Constructed ☐

Type of Shelter

Clothing/Coverings ☐

Waterproof ☐

Animal proof ☐

Sunproof ☐

Fire Started ☐

Food Inventory

Rations ☐

Water ☐

Hunting ☐

Fishing ☐

Foraging ☐

Journey

Distance Covered

Trail Markers Used

Landmarks Sighted

Animal Prints

Map Sketch

Lat. Long.

Party Member	Status	Injuries	Treatment

Date ______________

Conditions

Weather

Terrain

Shelter

Shelter Constructed ☐

Type of Shelter

Clothing/Coverings ☐

Waterproof ☐

Animal proof ☐

Sunproof ☐

Fire Started ☐

Food Inventory

Rations ☐

Water ☐

Hunting ☐

Fishing ☐

Foraging ☐

Journey

Distance Covered

Trail Markers Used

Landmarks Sighted

Animal Prints

Map Sketch

Lat.

Long.

Party Member	Status	Injuries	Treatment

Date

Conditions

Weather

Terrain

Food Inventory

Rations ☐

Water ☐

Hunting ☐

Fishing ☐

Foraging ☐

Journey

Distance Covered

Trail Markers Used

Landmarks Sighted

Animal Prints

Shelter

Shelter Constructed ☐

Type of Shelter

Clothing/Coverings ☐

Waterproof ☐

Animal proof ☐

Sunproof ☐

Fire Started ☐

Map Sketch

Lat. Long.

Party Member	Status	Injuries	Treatment

Date ____________

Conditions

Weather

Terrain

Shelter

Shelter Constructed ☐

Type of Shelter

Clothing/Coverings ☐

Waterproof ☐

Animal proof ☐

Sunproof ☐

Fire Started ☐

Food Inventory

Rations ☐

Water ☐

Hunting ☐

Fishing ☐

Foraging ☐

Journey

Distance Covered

Trail Markers Used

Landmarks Sighted

Animal Prints

Map Sketch

Lat. Long.

Party Member	Status	Injuries	Treatment

Date ____________

Conditions

Weather

Terrain

Shelter

Shelter Constructed ☐

Type of Shelter

Clothing/Coverings ☐

Waterproof ☐

Animal proof ☐

Sunproof ☐

Fire Started ☐

Food Inventory

Rations ☐

Water ☐

Hunting ☐

Fishing ☐

Foraging ☐

Journey

Distance Covered

Trail Markers Used

Landmarks Sighted

Animal Prints

Map Sketch

Lat. Long.

Party Member	Status	Injuries	Treatment

Date ______

Conditions

Weather

Terrain

Shelter

Shelter Constructed ☐

Type of Shelter

Clothing/Coverings ☐

Waterproof ☐

Animal proof ☐

Sunproof ☐

Fire Started ☐

Food Inventory

Rations ☐

Water ☐

Hunting ☐

Fishing ☐

Foraging ☐

Journey

Distance Covered

Trail Markers Used

Landmarks Sighted

Animal Prints

Map Sketch

Lat. Long.

Party Member	Status	Injuries	Treatment

Date

Conditions

Weather

Terrain

Shelter

Shelter Constructed ☐

Type of Shelter

Clothing/Coverings ☐

Waterproof ☐

Animal proof ☐

Sunproof ☐

Fire Started ☐

Food Inventory

Rations ☐

Water ☐

Hunting ☐

Fishing ☐

Foraging ☐

Journey

Distance Covered

Trail Markers Used

Landmarks Sighted

Animal Prints

Map Sketch

Lat. Long.

Party Member	Status	Injuries	Treatment

Date

Conditions

Weather

Terrain

Shelter

Shelter Constructed ☐

Type of Shelter

Clothing/Coverings ☐

Waterproof ☐

Animal proof ☐

Sunproof ☐

Fire Started ☐

Food Inventory

Rations ☐

Water ☐

Hunting ☐

Fishing ☐

Foraging ☐

Journey

Distance Covered

Trail Markers Used

Landmarks Sighted

Animal Prints

Map Sketch

Lat. Long.

Party Member	Status	Injuries	Treatment

Date

Conditions

Weather

Terrain

Shelter

Shelter Constructed ☐

Type of Shelter

Clothing/Coverings ☐

Waterproof ☐

Animal proof ☐

Sunproof ☐

Fire Started ☐

Food Inventory

Rations ☐

Water ☐

Hunting ☐

Fishing ☐

Foraging ☐

Journey

Distance Covered

Trail Markers Used

Landmarks Sighted

Animal Prints

Map Sketch

Lat. Long.

Party Member	Status	Injuries	Treatment

Date ______________

Conditions

Weather

Terrain

Shelter

Shelter Constructed ☐

Type of Shelter

Clothing/Coverings ☐

Waterproof ☐

Animal proof ☐

Sunproof ☐

Fire Started ☐

Food Inventory

Rations ☐

Water ☐

Hunting ☐

Fishing ☐

Foraging ☐

Journey

Distance Covered

Trail Markers Used

Landmarks Sighted

Animal Prints

Map Sketch

Lat. Long.

Party Member	Status	Injuries	Treatment

Date ____________

Conditions

Weather

Terrain

Shelter

Shelter Constructed ☐

Type of Shelter

Clothing/Coverings ☐

Waterproof ☐

Animal proof ☐

Sunproof ☐

Fire Started ☐

Food Inventory

Rations ☐

Water ☐

Hunting ☐

Fishing ☐

Foraging ☐

Journey

Distance Covered

Trail Markers Used

Landmarks Sighted

Animal Prints

Map Sketch

Lat. Long.

Party Member	Status	Injuries	Treatment

Date

Conditions

Weather

Terrain

Shelter

Shelter Constructed ☐

Type of Shelter

Clothing/Coverings ☐

Waterproof ☐

Animal proof ☐

Sunproof ☐

Fire Started ☐

Food Inventory

Rations ☐

Water ☐

Hunting ☐

Fishing ☐

Foraging ☐

Journey

Distance Covered

Trail Markers Used

Landmarks Sighted

Animal Prints

Map Sketch

Lat. Long.

Party Member	Status	Injuries	Treatment

Date

Conditions

Weather

Terrain

Food Inventory

Rations ☐

Water ☐

Hunting ☐

Fishing ☐

Foraging ☐

Journey

Distance Covered

Trail Markers Used

Landmarks Sighted

Animal Prints

Shelter

Shelter Constructed ☐

Type of Shelter

Clothing/Coverings ☐

Waterproof ☐

Animal proof ☐

Sunproof ☐

Fire Started ☐

Map Sketch

Lat. Long.

Party Member	Status	Injuries	Treatment

Date

Conditions

Weather

Terrain

Shelter

Shelter Constructed ☐

Type of Shelter

Clothing/Coverings ☐

Waterproof ☐

Animal proof ☐

Sunproof ☐

Fire Started ☐

Food Inventory

Rations ☐

Water ☐

Hunting ☐

Fishing ☐

Foraging ☐

Journey

Distance Covered

Trail Markers Used

Landmarks Sighted

Animal Prints

Map Sketch

Lat. Long.

Party Member	Status	Injuries	Treatment

Date

Conditions

Weather

Terrain

Shelter

Shelter Constructed ☐

Type of Shelter

Clothing/Coverings ☐

Waterproof ☐

Animal proof ☐

Sunproof ☐

Fire Started ☐

Food Inventory

Rations ☐

Water ☐

Hunting ☐

Fishing ☐

Foraging ☐

Journey

Distance Covered

Trail Markers Used

Landmarks Sighted

Animal Prints

Map Sketch

Lat. Long.

Party Member	Status	Injuries	Treatment

Date ____________

Conditions

Weather

Terrain

Shelter

Shelter Constructed ☐

Type of Shelter

Clothing/Coverings ☐

Waterproof ☐

Animal proof ☐

Sunproof ☐

Fire Started ☐

Food Inventory

Rations ☐

Water ☐

Hunting ☐

Fishing ☐

Foraging ☐

Journey

Distance Covered

Trail Markers Used

Landmarks Sighted

Animal Prints

Map Sketch

Lat. Long.

Party Member	Status	Injuries	Treatment

Date ______

Conditions

Weather

Terrain

Food Inventory

Rations ☐

Water ☐

Hunting ☐

Fishing ☐

Foraging ☐

Journey

Distance Covered

Trail Markers Used

Landmarks Sighted

Animal Prints

Shelter

Shelter Constructed ☐

Type of Shelter

Clothing/Coverings ☐

Waterproof ☐

Animal proof ☐

Sunproof ☐

Fire Started ☐

Map Sketch

Lat. Long.

Party Member	Status	Injuries	Treatment

Date

Conditions

Weather

Terrain

Food Inventory

Rations ☐

Water ☐

Hunting ☐

Fishing ☐

Foraging ☐

Journey

Distance Covered

Trail Markers Used

Landmarks Sighted

Animal Prints

Shelter

Shelter Constructed ☐

Type of Shelter

Clothing/Coverings ☐

Waterproof ☐

Animal proof ☐

Sunproof ☐

Fire Started ☐

Map Sketch

Lat. Long.

Party Member	Status	Injuries	Treatment

Date ______________

Conditions

Weather

Terrain

Shelter

Shelter Constructed ☐

Type of Shelter

Clothing/Coverings ☐

Waterproof ☐

Animal proof ☐

Sunproof ☐

Fire Started ☐

Food Inventory

Rations ☐

Water ☐

Hunting ☐

Fishing ☐

Foraging ☐

Journey

Distance Covered

Trail Markers Used

Landmarks Sighted

Animal Prints

Map Sketch

Lat.

Long.

Party Member	Status	Injuries	Treatment

Date

Conditions

Weather

Terrain

Food Inventory

Rations ☐

Water ☐

Hunting ☐

Fishing ☐

Foraging ☐

Journey

Distance Covered

Trail Markers Used

Landmarks Sighted

Animal Prints

Shelter

Shelter Constructed ☐

Type of Shelter

Clothing/Coverings ☐

Waterproof ☐

Animal proof ☐

Sunproof ☐

Fire Started ☐

Map Sketch

Lat. Long.

Party Member	Status	Injuries	Treatment

Date ____________

Conditions

Weather

Terrain

Shelter

Shelter Constructed ☐

Type of Shelter

Clothing/Coverings ☐

Waterproof ☐

Animal proof ☐

Sunproof ☐

Fire Started ☐

Food Inventory

Rations ☐

Water ☐

Hunting ☐

Fishing ☐

Foraging ☐

Journey

Distance Covered

Trail Markers Used

Landmarks Sighted

Animal Prints

Map Sketch

Lat. Long.

Party Member	Status	Injuries	Treatment

Date

Conditions

Weather

Terrain

Food Inventory

Rations ☐

Water ☐

Hunting ☐

Fishing ☐

Foraging ☐

Journey

Distance Covered

Trail Markers Used

Landmarks Sighted

Animal Prints

Shelter

Shelter Constructed ☐

Type of Shelter

Clothing/Coverings ☐

Waterproof ☐

Animal proof ☐

Sunproof ☐

Fire Started ☐

Map Sketch

Lat. Long.

Party Member	Status	Injuries	Treatment

Date ____________

Conditions

Weather

Terrain

Shelter

Shelter Constructed ☐

Type of Shelter

Clothing/Coverings ☐

Waterproof ☐

Animal proof ☐

Sunproof ☐

Fire Started ☐

Food Inventory

Rations ☐

Water ☐

Hunting ☐

Fishing ☐

Foraging ☐

Journey

Distance Covered

Trail Markers Used

Landmarks Sighted

Animal Prints

Map Sketch

Lat. Long.

Party Member	Status	Injuries	Treatment

Date

Conditions

Weather

Terrain

Shelter

Shelter Constructed ☐

Type of Shelter

Clothing/Coverings ☐

Waterproof ☐

Animal proof ☐

Sunproof ☐

Fire Started ☐

Food Inventory

Rations ☐

Water ☐

Hunting ☐

Fishing ☐

Foraging ☐

Journey

Distance Covered

Trail Markers Used

Landmarks Sighted

Animal Prints

Map Sketch

Lat.

Long.

Party Member	Status	Injuries	Treatment

Date

Conditions

Weather

Terrain

Shelter

Shelter Constructed ☐

Type of Shelter

Clothing/Coverings ☐

Waterproof ☐

Animal proof ☐

Sunproof ☐

Fire Started ☐

Food Inventory

Rations ☐

Water ☐

Hunting ☐

Fishing ☐

Foraging ☐

Journey

Distance Covered

Trail Markers Used

Landmarks Sighted

Animal Prints

Map Sketch

Lat. Long.

Party Member	Status	Injuries	Treatment

Date ______________

Conditions

Weather

Terrain

Shelter

Shelter Constructed ☐

Type of Shelter

Clothing/Coverings ☐

Waterproof ☐

Animal proof ☐

Sunproof ☐

Fire Started ☐

Food Inventory

Rations ☐

Water ☐

Hunting ☐

Fishing ☐

Foraging ☐

Journey

Distance Covered

Trail Markers Used

Landmarks Sighted

Animal Prints

Map Sketch

Lat. Long.

Party Member	Status	Injuries	Treatment

Date ____________

Conditions

Weather

Terrain

Shelter

Shelter Constructed ☐

Type of Shelter

Clothing/Coverings ☐

Waterproof ☐

Animal proof ☐

Sunproof ☐

Fire Started ☐

Food Inventory

Rations ☐

Water ☐

Hunting ☐

Fishing ☐

Foraging ☐

Journey

Distance Covered

Trail Markers Used

Landmarks Sighted

Animal Prints

Map Sketch

Lat. Long.

Party Member	Status	Injuries	Treatment

Date ______

Conditions

Weather

Terrain

Shelter

Shelter Constructed ☐

Type of Shelter

Clothing/Coverings ☐

Waterproof ☐

Animal proof ☐

Sunproof ☐

Fire Started ☐

Food Inventory

Rations ☐

Water ☐

Hunting ☐

Fishing ☐

Foraging ☐

Journey

Distance Covered

Trail Markers Used

Landmarks Sighted

Animal Prints

Map Sketch

Lat. Long.

Party Member	Status	Injuries	Treatment

Date

Conditions

Weather

Terrain

Shelter

Shelter Constructed ☐

Type of Shelter

Clothing/Coverings ☐

Waterproof ☐

Animal proof ☐

Sunproof ☐

Fire Started ☐

Food Inventory

Rations ☐

Water ☐

Hunting ☐

Fishing ☐

Foraging ☐

Journey

Distance Covered

Trail Markers Used

Landmarks Sighted

Animal Prints

Map Sketch

Lat. Long.

Party Member	Status	Injuries	Treatment

Date

Conditions

Weather

Terrain

Shelter

Shelter Constructed ☐

Type of Shelter

Clothing/Coverings ☐

Waterproof ☐

Animal proof ☐

Sunproof ☐

Fire Started ☐

Food Inventory

Rations ☐

Water ☐

Hunting ☐

Fishing ☐

Foraging ☐

Journey

Distance Covered

Trail Markers Used

Landmarks Sighted

Animal Prints

Map Sketch

Lat. Long.

Party Member	Status	Injuries	Treatment

Date

Conditions

Weather

Terrain

Food Inventory

Rations ☐

Water ☐

Hunting ☐

Fishing ☐

Foraging ☐

Journey

Distance Covered

Trail Markers Used

Landmarks Sighted

Animal Prints

Shelter

Shelter Constructed ☐

Type of Shelter

Clothing/Coverings ☐

Waterproof ☐

Animal proof ☐

Sunproof ☐

Fire Started ☐

Map Sketch

Lat. Long.

Party Member	Status	Injuries	Treatment

Date

Conditions

Weather

Terrain

Shelter

Shelter Constructed ☐

Type of Shelter

Clothing/Coverings ☐

Waterproof ☐

Animal proof ☐

Sunproof ☐

Fire Started ☐

Food Inventory

Rations ☐

Water ☐

Hunting ☐

Fishing ☐

Foraging ☐

Journey

Distance Covered

Trail Markers Used

Landmarks Sighted

Animal Prints

Map Sketch

Lat. Long.

Party Member	Status	Injuries	Treatment

Date

Conditions

Weather

Terrain

Shelter

Shelter Constructed ☐

Type of Shelter

Clothing/Coverings ☐

Waterproof ☐

Animal proof ☐

Sunproof ☐

Fire Started ☐

Food Inventory

Rations ☐

Water ☐

Hunting ☐

Fishing ☐

Foraging ☐

Journey

Distance Covered

Trail Markers Used

Landmarks Sighted

Animal Prints

Map Sketch

Lat. Long.

Party Member	Status	Injuries	Treatment

Date

Conditions

Weather

Terrain

Shelter

Shelter Constructed ☐

Type of Shelter

Clothing/Coverings ☐

Waterproof ☐

Animal proof ☐

Sunproof ☐

Fire Started ☐

Food Inventory

Rations ☐

Water ☐

Hunting ☐

Fishing ☐

Foraging ☐

Journey

Distance Covered

Trail Markers Used

Landmarks Sighted

Animal Prints

Map Sketch

Lat.

Long.

Party Member	Status	Injuries	Treatment

Date

Conditions

Weather

Terrain

Shelter

Shelter Constructed ☐

Type of Shelter

Clothing/Coverings ☐

Waterproof ☐

Animal proof ☐

Sunproof ☐

Fire Started ☐

Food Inventory

Rations ☐

Water ☐

Hunting ☐

Fishing ☐

Foraging ☐

Journey

Distance Covered

Trail Markers Used

Landmarks Sighted

Animal Prints

Map Sketch

Lat. Long.

Party Member	Status	Injuries	Treatment

www.ingramcontent.com/pod-product-compliance
Lightning Source LLC
LaVergne TN
LVHW060140080526
838202LV00049B/4036
* 9 7 8 3 3 4 7 0 2 9 2 5 5 *